Be Patient.

Julie P.

# 25 Ways to Encourage Good Behavior

## with

## More Discipline, Less Punishment

by Julie Prescott

*Single Parent Wisdom series*

Wynot Publications • Corning, Iowa

This book is intended to provide helpful and informative material on the subjects addressed. It is sold with the understanding that the author and contributors are not engaged in rendering medical, legal, financial, psychiatric, or any other kind of professional services. The reader should consult competent professionals regarding serious problems.

For more information contact:
        Wynot Publications
        P.O. Box 477
        Corning, IA 50841-0477
        http://www.singleparentwisdom.com
        (712) 898-0433


ISBN 978-0-9821326-0-9
Library of Congress Control Number: 2009924392


Printed in the United States of America
10 9 8 7 6 5 4 3 2 1

# In this book...

Introduction ............................................................................ 1

#1 Take Care of Problems Now, Not Later .................................. 7

#2 Provide Structure and Boundaries .................................... 8

#3 Set Positive, Reachable Goals ......................................... 15

#4 Find Your Strength ........................................................ 18

#5 Be More Positive and Less Negative .............................. 19

#6 Praise, Encourage, Appreciate ...................................... 21

#7 Be Patient; Be Affectionate ........................................... 24

#8 Distract or Redirect ....................................................... 24

#9 Remove Yourself from the Situation ............................... 25

#10 Role-play ..................................................................... 26

#11 Set an Example; Be a Role Model .................................. 27

#12 Apologize; Be Forgiving ................................................ 27

#13 Warn; Give Second Chances ........................................ 28

#14 Offer Choices ............................................................... 30

#15 Be Fair; Be Respectful .................................................. 32

#16 Use Humor Appropriately, not Harshly ......................... 33

#17 Encourage Responsibility ............................................. 33

#18 Be Predictable, Be Consistent ...................................... 34

#19 Don't Bribe; Seldom Use Rewards ................................ 36

#20 Instill Incentives to Encourage Good Behavior ...... 36

Establish Consequences for Incorrect Behavior .......... 37

#21 Listen To Your Child First, Then Talk ............................. 42

#22 Don't Punish, Slap, Spank, or Hit ................................. 46

#23 Love Your Child Unconditionally ................................... 48

#24 Involve the Other Parent, When Possible ..................... 49

#25 Ask For Help Until You Get It ........................................ 49

Appendix: Consequences ................................................. 52

Appendix: Time-Outs ........................................................ 54

Appendix: "Our Family" Notebook ..................................... 56

Index .................................................................................. 57

Bibliography ....................................................................... 59

How to Order More Single Parent Wisdom Books ......... 60

AUTHOR'S NOTE: The use of 'he' and 'she' alternates. The
name "Chris" substitutes for "child" representing both a male
and female child from ages 2 to 18.

Many of the names of parents contributing comments have been
changed to protect their children's identity, including the author.

Recommended website URL addresses are provided for
continued research. If you find that a URL doesn't work, please
e-mail us at info@singleparentwisdom.com to update our
information.

# Introduction

Behavior is a reaction to an event, a word, a thought, an emotion, a sound, or a feeling. It can be an automatic response made quickly and rationally, such as running at the sound of an explosion. Or it can be a calculated action.

When a 10-year-old stomps his feet after Dad says, "No!" he has chosen that action for best effect. Certain habitual or genetic behavior, such as an active child in a quiet, modest family, or a shy child in a noisy, busy family, takes effort for all to adapt to each other.

Good behavior is a socially acceptable reaction. We teach our children how to behave by our actions and words. At times we accidentally reinforce misbehavior.

I was a single parent for 11 years. Now that my children are adults, I am seeking the answers to questions about parenting to help young parents now faced with the parenting puzzle. I interview and question parents like me — single parents when their children were young, but now their children are grown. Who better to tell us what works and what does not than solo parents who have made all of the decisions and handled all of the responsibility. From our experiences we have learned when to listen to the experts, realize when we actually do know best, choose to let the matter slide, and when to seek help. We are wiser. We are your **SPWISDOM** support group.

## Key points made by the solo parents are easy to locate with these designs:

### Be Consistent

Be consistent about the BIG problems. Teach the values that are important to you. Consistency provides stability and structure that your children need. Have faith in your judgment.

When you are in doubt, there are books, workshops, and people to talk with about parenting choices.

You will naturally be inconsistent about the little stuff, depending on how much energy you have that day.

## Be Patient & Loving

Your child needs to know that you love her now and forever. Everyday, tell and show your child that she is important in your life.

## Time is Short

✓ Choose your battles.
✓ Do your best.
✓ Your child will be an adult before you know it.

## Be Age-Appropriate with your Child

As the parent or guardian you need to be aware of what your child can handle at her current physical, social, emotional, and intellectual level. Expecting a child to handle challenges beyond her ability may frustrate, scare, upset, confuse, or harm her. Be careful to not push your child too much. Don't let others push her, either.

The comments in this book are not designated for a certain age. You will need to decide when a suggestion or tip is "age-appropriate" to apply to your child. Some advice is meant for preschoolers but not for teens, and vice versa.

For a better understanding of what to expect at what age, visit the SINGLE PARENT WISDOM website at www.singleparentwisdom.com, Child Development.

## Reduce the Chaos

Don't accept chaos as a natural part of your life. Change something. Aim for a calm household. Have structure in your days. Life gets better with less chaos.

### Be a Role Model

Every now and then you will be reminded that you are your child's number one role model. She watches everything you do and say. Make her proud!

### Live in the Present
### — Plan for the Future

As philosopher Deepak Chopra reminds us:

**You may not have been responsible for your heritage, but you are responsible for your future.**

Our children put up with our past:

➤ A dysfunctional relationship with our own parents
➤ Dissatisfaction with goals we set when young that have not been achieved
➤ Divorce or separation, or lack of a second parent in the home
➤ Lack of money to buy the perfect house or car

If you regret the past, then stop reliving it. Rather than wishing things were different, accept the life you have now — and move forward! Your child lives for today with hopes for the future. Join her.

### And one from me: Celebrate!

There are not enough celebrations. In the really old days (even before I was born), a birthday was a big celebration as people struggled to live each year.

• There was too much disease and no antibiotics.
• Childbirth was no picnic.
• Wolves actually might eat you.
• If you broke a leg or got shot, good luck surviving that!
• Eyeglasses were not that effective. I would have surely walked off a cliff.

*Celebrate!* Each morning a small child wakes filled with excitement for a new day. Enjoy their enthusiasm.

**There are so many possibilities to celebrate:**
☺ The first day of the month
☺ The first day of school
☺ The last day of school
☺ Child's first paying job
☺ Your new job
☺ Child's first attempt at fixing supper
☺ Your best attempt at fixing supper
☺ Child's first two-wheeled bicycle
☺ Teen's first car
☺ You or your child learning a new skill
What other days can your child and you celebrate?
*Have fun!*

## Introducing Chris

Chris can be a boy or a girl. He or she is sometimes a 2-year-old, other times 17, and everything in-between. He/she might attend preschool, elementary school, middle or high school. Your child is our Chris.

Just as with Chris, the parents or guardians are sometimes a he and sometimes a she. You'll find helpful tips, whether you are a grandparent, uncle, neighbor, concerned friend, or future parent.

Our Chris is not a baby. This book concentrates on the ages of 2 and beyond. Babies require love, patience, and attentive care whether you are single or married. A listing of books and websites on baby care can be found on the SINGLE PARENT WISDOM website at www. singleparentwisdom.com, Resources.

## In this book...

You will find common sense, tried-n-true methods, new ideas, plus advice from experts.

Books, studies, newsletters, and magazines are scoured to bring you current information on parenting. Workshops, classes and seminars are attended. Interviews are conducted and questionnaires completed.

Some information stated is just plain common sense. Validation — having others agree that you are doing the right thing is sometimes all the support you may need. Some information will be new to you.

Conflicting advice is included. Since every family situation is unique, what works for one family may not work for another. Try different ideas. There is no one way to raise a child.

If you have a specific problem or need, there are many resources available on the **SINGLE PARENT WISDOM** website at www.singleparentwisdom.com, Resources.

## One final question asked of our experienced SPWISDOM support group:

## If you knew then what you know now what would you change?

You will find those answers by this design —

Please learn from our mistakes and our success. This is the wisdom we share.

There is a great future for your children and for you. Gather the advice you feel you need. Use it and then enjoy each day as it comes. Your children will be young for only a short while.

Poet Robert Browning was right:

## The best is yet to be.

# 25 Ways to Encourage Good Behavior
## with
## More Discipline & Less Punishment

### #1 Take Care of Problems Now, Not Later

Do you keep quiet when you witness misdeeds and then lump the memories of misbehavior into one angry outburst? Allen Elkin, *Stress Management for Dummies®*, describes this as Kitchen-Sinking a person. It's not fair. Children prefer fair. If you didn't correct the action when it happened, how was she to know that you really cared?

**TODAY!**
Live
in the
Present

> "Discipline works best when it's immediate, mild, and brief, because it's then associated with the transgression and doesn't breed more anger and resentment."
> Nancy Shute, "Good Parents, Bad Results"
> *U.S. News & World Report*

### Don't catastrophize

- The world won't end if the trash doesn't make it to the curb this week.
- Your child isn't condemned to a life in prison if she steals one piece of candy. Discuss the theft and have consequences for wrong choices of behavior.
  (See **#20**, page 36 and the APPENDIX on page 53.)
- The roof won't fall in if your child disagrees with you about a House Rule. Say, "I can understand how you might feel that way." Consider her opinion and change the rule, or not.

## #2 Provide Structure and Boundaries

Your home needs to be…

➢ a place where she can tell you anything,
➢ a place where she knows she's always loved,
➢ a place where she knows the rules and knows what to expect,
➢ a place where she is respected and not laughed at, and
➢ especially, a place where chaos doesn't happen.

Your child will feel more secure if there is structure in the family. Set meal times, curfews and bedtimes. Guidelines for acceptable behavior define what is okay and not okay to do. Boundaries include a 5-year-old not allowed to cross the street alone to a teen refusing to drink alcohol.

**Our SPWISDOM support group members share how they established structure in their homes**

*I sent them to their room without my screaming about the issues. After an hour or so, when I was calmer, I dealt with the issues and made ground rules to prevent future occurrences.*

Ann, mother of 4

*My boys were over-active and had trouble concentrating in school. I demanded strict, structured teachers.*

Karen, mother of 2 boys

*There were rules of conduct which they were pretty good at following, except for fighting with each other. If they wanted me to bend a rule they had to convince me there was a good reason, and occasionally I did.*

Clyde, father of 2

> We give our children everything, then we wonder why they expect everything.
>
> Stan Chartier
> parent

*The only boundary I ever set was I never allowed them to hit each other. When it happened, and it did, they were given a strict warning: "That behavior isn't tolerated." I didn't have to spank or strike them to let them know I meant business.*

Tom, father of 3

*He had to maintain some rules such as curfew. He always had to test the waters, though. When he was younger, we always had open communication. As a teenager he wanted to keep things from me.*                    Dody, mother of a boy

*I expected my sons to be dependable, honest, and morally pure and to avoid any activity that could appear to be wrong.*
                                        Linda, mother of 3 boys

*Rules were set for time limits at night, dating and driving. No cars of their own until after high school, and they helped pay for them.*                                    John, father of 4

*Before my husband died, the rules were specific. When I was alone, I didn't handle the grief very well and behavior problems did erupt.*                                Hester, mother of 5
After a tragedy or family change, try to keep the rules similar to before the change. We benefit from constants in our life.

*If I could change things I would have been much stricter and not so worried about their emotions all the time. I wouldn't have let them manipulate me the way they did. I wanted so bad to make sure they wouldn't have "childhood issues" as adults. Now I know they have them no matter what. I should have demanded respect. The older two reassure me I did a "good job" being a mom and that feels good. I know I did the best I could at the time.*
                                        Debra, mother of 3 boys

Our children need to understand and follow directions, respect us (adults), follow the schedules set for them, and act reasonably intelligent in public, submits Phil McGraw, *Family First.*

## Set House Rules

What are the rules in your home? Do you need to establish a few more to put limits on certain behaviors?

**In our home, the rules are...**
- ✓ Children don't light matches
- ✓ Children don't use the stove
- ✓ No biting, kicking, hitting or fighting
- ✓ Don't take someone else's toys
- ✓ No bad words like swearing, name-calling, or the phrase "Shut up"
- ✓ School Night curfew (to be in the house) is ___p.m.; Bedtime is ___p.m.
- ✓ Weekend Night curfew (to be in the house) is ___p.m.; Bedtime is ___p.m.
- ✓ No friends in the house if a parent isn't home
- ✓ Assigned chores to be done by Saturday noon
- ✓ Get an agreement to switch the TV channel with the other people watching
- ✓ Don't throw balls inside the house

**And when a rule is broken, the consequence is...**

The consequence for breaking a House Rule needs to be fair and applied as a matter-of-fact. Everyone, including mom and dad, need to follow the rules and show consideration for each other.

If your child refuses to follow any rules it's okay to be exasperated, but take action. Sit down with your child and discuss the civilized society we live in together. There are reasons for rules. Curfews are for safety and protection. Not hitting or biting shows courtesy and consideration for each other. We are civilized and need to live together cooperatively. Discuss with your child how life would be different if everyone just did what they wanted all the time. *Examples*:
- ☹ When drivers and pedestrians ignore stop signs, vehicles crash into each other. People get hurt.
- ☹ When chores are not done, the house fills up with dirty

dishes and unwashed clothes. Bugs are everywhere. No one visits because of the smells. Big animals are attracted to the smells in our kitchen and on our smelly bodies. Bears break into the house to eat our trash.

When fighting breaks out, remind them of the rules. Then walk away. To help enforce the rules list them on a sheet of paper and hang it by the kitchen calendar.

PARENT: *Sorry, dear, I'd love to let you watch TV tonight, but you broke a House Rule last night and you know the consequence is no TV for (number of) hours.*

School psychologist Sal Severe divulges in *How to Behave So Your Children Will, Too!*
Rules are expectations, and expectations guide children's decision making. There are three factors to consider when developing expectations or rules. Expectations must be **specific**, **reasonable**, and **enforceable**.

**Specific** — "Bedroom cleaned every Saturday morning before noon."
*Checklist*:

- ☐ All dirty clothes put in the laundry basket.
- ☐ All furniture dusted and polished.
- ☐ Carpet vacuumed.
- ☐ Sheets changed.
- ☐ All toys in toy box.
- ☐ All clean clothes put away.

**Reasonable** — Is this something your child at her age can do?

**Enforceable** — You can tell by looking if the tasks are completed. If one or two of the items on the checklist haven't been completed, the child must work on that before she continues with her day.

Meet Chris, a boy or a girl, young or old, your child.

Telling your child, "Clean your room," is unclear. Together make a checklist of what that means. All toys and books need a storage place such as on a shelf, drawer, box, closet, and/or under-her-bed. Help your child find a specific place for everything. Add labels or pictures to the shelves and boxes, such as Balls, Games, Books, Dolls.

☞ Explain the rules. Be brief. No lectures. Be a parent, not a friend. Your children will not like all the decisions you make. That's normal. Have rules to guide them. Share mutual respect.

When a child does something wrong and says, "I didn't know," discuss how you just can't list every correct behavior you expect. Explain that you set a few rules and anticipate Chris can think for herself if other possible actions are okay or not okay.

## Be precise in your instructions, please

Chris needs to understand your rules from her current ability to interpret your commands. When I was young, I was punished for not "staying in my yard" after supper. Since I was playing in the driveway behind the garage, my parents couldn't see me. I was sure the driveway was part of our yard. I knew it was our property. Had my parents stated, "Stay where we can see you from the kitchen window," I would have done just that. I simply interpreted the order to keep me from wandering around the neighborhood. Be precise.

Dr. Kevin Leman, *Parenthood Without Hassles*, asked children how many times their parents tell them to do something before they know they have to listen. Unanimously, they said 3 times. How many times do you repeat yourself before your child knows it's the final time? What do you do differently so she knows this is it? Do that earlier. Warn her that you are only going to tell her once — then only tell her once.

If Chris can't do anything right to please you and follow the simplest rules, revisit your list of rules. Make sure they are age-appropriate. A toddler cannot be expected to clean her room. Your teen may be taller than you, but does not have the judgment of an adult. Eliminate some rules, put the remaining rules in order of importance, and then encourage Chris to follow just one rule. When she does, compliment her. Children really do want to please parents.

### This is just a test!

Children constantly test us to see if the boundaries or rules have changed. If you haven't set any rules, then you are

in for even more testing. They need to know that you care so much about them that you want to keep them out of harm's way. You set guidelines to help them make the right choices. Then they expect you to be the enforcer to prove that they are good rules.

When I take a small child in my van for the first time, the child runs between the seats escaping to the back. Besides being fun to the child, it is a test to see how I will react.

I calmly say, "Get into the car seat please. We have to leave, now."

If that doesn't get immediate results, I add with a cheery voice, "We can play later."

A child understands that. He learns I don't yell easily, and I like to play, too. To get mad at the child for not climbing into his seat would be a waste of my energy and would not benefit the child, except to tell him that I get mad easily. (Although I admit I did as a young parent.)

☞ Use Family Meetings to set Guidelines and House Rules. For more information on holding Family Meetings, see #104 *How to Make Parental Decisions*, page 60.

### Provide safety and security

Psychologist James Dobson, *Focus on the Family*, relates:

> There is security in defined limits. They need
> to know precisely what the rules are and who's
> available to enforce them. Whenever a strong-willed
> child senses that the boundaries may have moved,
> or that his or her parents may have lost their
> nerve, the child will often start a fight just to test
> the limits again. Children may not admit that they
> want you to be the boss, but they breathe easier
> when you prove that you are.

Simplicity guru Elaine St. James, *Simplify Your Life with Kids*, clarifies:

> This sense of security comes from consistency. If
> kids aren't wary of the mood you're in, they can
> confide in you. If they know you won't yell, they
> can confess their mistakes. If they know you'll
> sympathize, they'll cry on your shoulder. If they
> know you'll listen, they'll tell you about their
> hopes and dreams (and maybe even tell you
> what they did in school today).

### Set physical boundaries

At a behavior workshop, a parent complained about her children leaving the yard and wandering to the street. Another parent offered this suggestion: She and her children threw apples into the busy street. Then they sat curbside to watch. Cars drove over the apples, smashing them. The mother explained to her children that cars are big, heavy machines that cannot stop easily. Graphic? Somewhat. Effective? Yes. *Caution*: Don't try this with a fearful child.

At that same workshop, another parent stated that she sprayed paint on the trees between the yard and the street. This showed the children their stopping point.

Have consequences for breaking the House Rules you teach them. See Appendix Consequences, page 52.

### #3 Set Positive, Reachable Goals

Make a list of behaviors that you want Chris to improve or do less.

➢  Chris will be on time for supper.
➢  Chris will not call his sister names.
➢  Chris will _____

Select one or two to work on for now. Start out with something that has the possibility of success. Don't start with the biggest problem.

### For young Chris, make a chart

*He initially would play at the supper table until I took a Behavior Modification course and made him my project. In the course you decide what behavior is going to be rewarded with points. After a large number of points are achieved a large reward is won (such as going to the movie). You post all this information on a chart and put stars for successes.*
*It worked!*                                    Patricia, mother of a boy

Remember when the teacher put stars on your paper, or better yet on a poster that the whole class could see? Stars were awarded for attendance, turning in homework, or good work.

On a chart, list just a couple behaviors that need improvement. Try to keep a positive tone, for example, #1 Chris makes his bed every morning; #2 Chris will be on time for supper. For each day that you see Chris doing the correct behavior, he receives a sticker on the chart.

Count up the stickers for the day, and he receives a special incentive — more time for bedtime stories, video games, or outside play. Ask Chris what he wants to work towards for getting a sticker for the day. Food isn't a good reward. Mark the chart only for correct behavior, not misbehavior — your child doesn't need the negative reminder. Have a bigger reward for a good week.

Continue the chart. Keep the same behaviors if there is still room for improvement, or add a new behavior to

improve. Encourage Chris by telling him that you know he can learn to follow these rules.

For older Chris, each sticker is worth a point. Points add up to special privileges, such as a ride to the mall, a movie, an overnight guest, or a slumber party. Keep an older child's chart out of sight from visitors (especially his friends). No need to embarrass or humiliate anyone. Keep it in the "Our Family" notebook (see page 56).

## Checklists make tasks easier

Try checklists for a child that needs the task broken down into smaller pieces such as bedtime, her morning routine or household chores. School psychologist Sal Severe suggests to make a list of the task in simple steps on a piece of paper. Either you or the child place a checkmark by each step as it is completed. Whether you include rewards is your choice. Know what motivates your child. Some parents choose not to reward for simple everyday tasks.

## Contracts work well with teens

Write a contract between teen Chris and you to encourage correct behavior. List the specific behavior you want your child to show, such as Chris will be in the house at 6 p.m. (on time for supper). Be precise. Include a consequence if misbehavior (he is late) occurs instead. Try the contract for a week or two. If it works, try another improvement. Be sure to tell Chris that you are proud of him for being on time for supper each day (the new behavior).

☞ Discuss the Chart, Checklist or Contract with Chris. Involve him. Talk about it at the Family Meeting. For more information on holding Family Meetings, see #104 *How to Make Parental Decisions*, page 60.

### Teach appropriate behavior

What is appropriate for your child at his current age? Are different behaviors acceptable at different times?

✓ Chris can sit quietly for short periods of time if he is at least 4 years old.

✓ Chris can learn to not interrupt people when they are talking by quietly letting them know he wants to talk to them and then waiting his turn.

✓ Chris can eat his food without making his sister gag.

✓ Chris can avoid punching his sister when she walks by.

**Inside the house?** Can Chris be wild and loud in the house when no one is sleeping or on the phone?

**At mealtime?** Chris needs to calm down so he can eat his food. Lively dinner conversation is okay, but getting out of his chair is not.

**At bedtime?** Chris needs to calm himself so he can fall asleep easily.

**At Grandma's?** Chris needs to be respectful of older people. Sudden actions and loud noises might make Grandma nervous. Are there precious knick-knacks that need to be guarded from active children?

**At church?** We use our quiet voices and don't run around (in most churches).

**Outside?** That's where we yell, run and jump.

✓ We don't run into the street. There might be traffic.

✓ We don't throw things at passing cars. We don't litter.

**At school?** Chris needs to be respectful to the teachers and cooperative to classmates. On the playground he can run around, but in the classroom he needs to stay in his seat. He needs to keep his hands to himself. He needs to listen and not talk sassy to the teacher.

**In a store?** Chris should stay by your side.

These appropriate behaviors make Chris nicer to be around for you and help him keep friends. Nobody likes a child who bites, throws tantrums, lies or gossips, to name a few bad behaviors. Self control is important to learn and use.

☞ We live in a social world. Self control is rewarded. Respecting society's system, whether it is the family, school, job, or the community, will benefit Chris.

## Even misbehavior has a goal

Chris is naturally curious, insecure, easily frustrated, and tempted. Did he misbehave because he wants your attention? Perhaps he's bored. Or he didn't understand that you were serious about "that" rule. Is he frustrated because he can't physically or mentally do what he is trying to do? Did he take the clock apart to see how it worked? Did he know he shouldn't?

If your child is angry at you, he may want to make you mad for revenge, warns Dr. Severe. He'll do something that assures him you will get angry, if not explode. How wonderful. How easy. What control. Your child believes it's worth the possible punishment.

Every Sunday, your family eats dinner at Grandma's house. (Nice tradition.) This time, Chris does something to make you ground him. Oh, too bad, he can't go. Have an appropriate consequence for his choice of misbehavior that is not too lenient, not too harsh, and doesn't actually end up rewarding him. (See **#20**, page 36 and **APPENDIX CONSEQUENCES**, page 52.)

## #4 Find Your Strength

We're not talking muscles. You need fortitude — the strength to be calm and patient, to go to work every day and come home, to greet your child with a smile, and to forget your aching feet.

A common statement by busy, overworked, stressed parents: **"I can't deal with this right now!"**

Become a strong parent. Get plenty of sleep. Eat more protein, fresh vegetables and fruit, and less caffeine and carbohydrates. Strive to live within your income for less stress.

You need to be strong and consistent when trying to change behavior. Changes don't happen overnight. If you are not assertive, have low self esteem, or experience depression, then seek help to be the best parent you can be for Chris. Take classes or read self-help books to improve your outlook. Tell your doctor if you are depressed.

## #5 Be More Positive and Less Negative

Although it's easy to find the negative in most situations, your life will improve if you develop a more positive outlook. Studies show positive people generally live a longer, happier life.

To fight my natural inclination to think negatively, I read books, listen to tapes, attend seminars, and remind myself through Self Talk to be positive. Surround yourself with "Yes-I-can" people instead of the "It-will-never-work" folks. Their optimism might rub off on you. Marrying my "Mr. Positive" Husband helped me.

In *Keeping Life Simple*, Karen Levine remarks, "…if we watch our kids with the feeling that any moment might bring a catastrophe, we lose the pleasure of the moment."

### What does your Self Talk sound like?

We judge, assess, praise, criticize, encourage, disapprove, tell ourselves everything will be fine, and also occasionally tell ourselves this is the end of the world.

Every chance you get, tell your children what they're doing right. As Dr. Phil points out in *Family First*, it is vital that children know they are good at something and build on that, instead of constantly being reminded what they can't do.

> The average child receives 400 negative comments a day compared to only 32 positive ones.
>
> Kathryn Kvols
> "Redirecting Children's Behavior"

Sally Koslow, "Surprising Secrets to Unshakeable Confidence" (*Reader's Digest*) illustrates:

> Negative feedback undermines anyone's belief in his or her ability to succeed. But if you can hold on to a winning attitude, you'll make a greater effort and also create positive momentum. Confident people inspire others; opportunities seem to come their way more often. They become magnets for success.

Leave the negative talk to restaurant critics who warn us of a really lousy place to eat. Hopefully, they can find something positive to say, such as, "Great atmosphere, helpful staff, and look at those clean spoons!"

## In the heat of the moment, choose words wisely

Remove "I told you so!" from your vocabulary. It may make you feel better for a short time, but it will anger or disappoint Chris, harming your relationship. Other phrases to avoid:

➤ *Why aren't you as smart as your brother?*
➤ *You are such a bad child.*
➤ *No! No! No!*

> Applaud.
> Don't "Boo."

Do you find yourself saying "No!" often? Use positive statements: "Yes, we'll do that sometime," or "Wouldn't that be fun?" If all a child hears is no, she will start to ignore you and do what she wants to do.

## Let Chris vent, for awhile

We state a problem out loud to help find the words that lead to a better understanding of the dilemma. If Chris makes the same negative comments over and over, suggest she find a solution or a way of accepting it, rather than complaining all the time. If you have any ideas, ask her if she wants to hear your suggestion. Otherwise, tell her, "I'm sure you can find a solution." Then tell her you don't want to hear about it anymore.

☞ That is as long as it is not something illegal or immoral and she is old enough to solve the problem or accept the situation.

☞ Constantly hearing negative talk about something you have no control over doesn't benefit you in any way, and wears on your outlook. Chris needs to be pro-active and search for a solution to problems.

☞ For problem solving tips, see #104 How to Make Parental Decisions, page 60.

## #6 Praise, Encourage, Appreciate

✓ Use praise sincerely, immediately, and directly.
✓ Tell your child you appreciate his efforts.
✓ Use encouragement often.

**Praise a child for a job well done. Consider the child's ability and not yours.**

☺ You changed your grade from a D to a C — way to go!
☺ Well done ☺ Remarkable ☺ I knew you could do it!
☺ I am proud of you for sticking with it until the job was done ☺ You figured it out ☺ What an imagination ☺
*Be careful*: Use sparingly and sincerely. Praise the specific act, not the child in general.

**Show appreciation for your child.**

✓ "I enjoy watching you play so nicely with sissy."
✓ "I appreciate that you took care of the dishes."
✓ "The living room looks so nice with your toys put away."

*Use often.* Appreciation encourages cooperation and the feeling of self-satisfaction and being part of the team, a sense of family.

**Show encouragement to a child while doing a task.**

☺ "What do you think of your work so far?"
☺ "If you're not happy with it, how can you do it differently or better?"
☺ "I like the colors you've chosen."
☺ "It looks to me like you really understand this homework assignment."

Properly used, encouraging words help Chris look inside himself to seek self-satisfaction. They also show that you notice what Chris does.

We exclaim with delight when our baby grasps our finger. We brag to relatives and neighbors her accomplishments from rolling over to walking. It goes downhill from there. Once the child can walk, she touch and grabs things. We stop praising and start saying, "No-no!" We continue to scold our little one to protect her or protect our stuff.

**Let's respond again to success:**
- School accomplishment — Completes all the assignments this semester.
- Physical accomplishments — Fewer scraped knees. Masters the chin-up.
- Social accomplishments — A kind gesture shown to a sister or neighbor.

     **Compliment the little things, scold less.**

### Pay attention when good behavior happens!

One day I had to stop at a store on the way home. I just sat in the car in the parking lot for awhile as my two children were getting antsy in the backseat. I was tired from my day of work.

Calmly I looked directly at my boy and girl and told them, "We are going into that store. We need to buy one thing. You will walk beside me and behave like a perfect gentleman and young lady. Then we will get in the car and go home."

No promises of treats and none bought. I did tell them what behavior I expected, plus how long the shopping might take. You and I may know it will be a quick stop, but the children are sure it will be a long, drawn out experience that's no fun. Best of all, I said we would go home soon. After a full day at child care, home was where they wanted to be. I still remember that shopping experience was better than any other, before or since.

Years later, I shared that recollection at a behavior workshop. The leader asked, "Did you compliment your children after you left the store?" Uh, no. I was proud of my children for following my instructions, but didn't tell them. By not sincerely praising them, I showed them I didn't appreciate their efforts. That explains why I don't remember it happening again. No wisdom learned that day.

> If you want cooperation, be cooperative.
>
> Don Dinkmeyer and Gary D. McKay "Parenting Teenagers"

## Children want to be considerate

Dr. Thomas Gordon in his book, *Parent Effectiveness Training*, offers:

> Children, not unlike adults, often don't know how their behavior affects others. In the pursuit of their own goals they are often totally unaware of the impact their behavior might have. Once they are told, they usually want to be more considerate.

*For example*: Chris gets so wrapped up in the game he's playing that he doesn't realize his loud talk bothers his brother watching television nearby. In some households this would erupt into a fight. Before the fight is even considered, teach your children how to talk nicely to each other to say what they need.

## Encourage teamwork

Assign a project that siblings must do together.

*Example*: Peel potatoes for supper, wash dishes after supper,

 rake the yard, empty wastebaskets into a trash bag and take to the trash bin, walk the dog, entertain baby sister for 20 minutes, help each other with vocabulary lists for 20 minutes, bake a cake for Grandma's birthday, or work on a hobby. By working together peacefully responsibilities are shared, others' talents are noticed, and hopefully cooperation gets the task done.

No siblings? Then the two of you can find projects to do together.

*Family Pastimes* game makers specialize in games to teach cooperation instead of competition. Games are available for all age groups, from paper games to board games and more at the website www.familypastimes.com.

### #7 Be Patient; Be Affectionate

When correcting a behavior that has been present for some time be patient, forewarns Dr. Severe. It may be weeks before you see any improvement.

*When a small child is angry and out of control, wrap your arms around him and talk soothingly. Say, "I understand. You're upset. It will get better."* Jeff, father of 2

Touch your child every day. Give a hug, pat her back, stroke her hair, hold her hand, or touch her arm. The simple act of a loving touch says, "You're okay."

When a child breaks a rule or misbehaves, she needs to know you still love her.

"Kindness is a language we all understand.
The blind can see it
and the deaf can hear it."

Mother Theresa

### #8 Distract or Redirect

A toddler can be picked up and removed from a problem situation. Young children have short attention spans and can be easily distracted. An older child needs to be redirected. Say, "That's not appropriate behavior. Find something else to do or go outside."

You set the guidelines by telling Chris what is right and what is wrong. He's not born with that knowledge. If you're not sure about right and wrong, seek guidance.

Redirect older Chris to work on a hobby or craft project, or to do something physical such as shoot baskets, or go for a run or a walk. Help him immerse himself in something so he will not think about misbehaving.

## #9 Remove Yourself from the Situation

If you feel overwhelmed or too upset by the situation, then mentally remove yourself for a few minutes by stating the alphabet calmly, slowly and out loud. Or leave the room. Tell Chris the two of you will discuss a consequence for the behavior later.

➤ Go to your room.
➤ Listen to music.
➤ Go for a walk (if Chris is old enough to be left alone).
➤ Plan your dream vacation.

☞ For more ideas, see *Parents! Take Care of Yourself*, page 60.

### Take a breather

You may have heard of the "Count to 10" rule. Basically, it's time to think and calm down. Try this method before disciplining Chris (as long as nothing is burning or flooding and no one is bleeding).

Sit or stand up straight. Throw your shoulders back. Then inhale deeply through your nose with your mouth closed, puffing out your chest. Exhale slowly through your mouth. Do this 8 to 10 times.

This gives you a chance to clear your head and think about what you're going to do next, instead of reacting with a slap to the child's face. Now with more oxygen in your brain the outlook might look less dim.

**Use Plain Talk.** Instead of listening to your whiny, possibly foul-mouthed child, just tell her: "I'm tired of this behavior. Find a better way to talk to me." Then walk away. Chris now has the responsibility to change her approach if she wants to be heard.

"Stop yelling all the time," my doctor said. I thought I lost my voice due to laryngitis.

A common reaction to frustration is to raise your voice. The louder you talk and the more often you talk in a loud voice, the sooner your children will learn to tune you out. Do not yell unless the house is on fire or they are about to be hit by a car. Their response time will improve greatly and they will know when you do yell it is of the utmost importance. (To get them to clear the table faster or pick up their toys isn't worth yelling about. What is really making you angry?)

In *SOS Help for Parents*, Dr. Lynn Clark divulges,
> Avoid expressing intense anger when you use correction. Your child should believe that she got corrected because she behaved badly and not because you got angry.

## #10 Role-play

Help Chris learn to handle new situations before they happen. Use puppets or take turns playing different characters. Create a pretend script of what might happen. This not only works well before a child's surgery, first dentist visit, or new school, but it also works for *Stranger Beware*, travel to a new place, difficulty with a certain person, interview for a job, and more.

Even adults often run different scenarios through their heads when faced with new situations or problems: "How will my co-workers react if I say this at the meeting tomorrow?"

**Role-play these scenarios with Chris:**
- ✓ Something happens that makes Chris mad. How does he calm himself down?
- ✓ Someone bullies Chris at school.
- ✓ A friend encourages him to steal a candy bar.
- ✓ He is offered a cigarette (or worse).

When Chris and you constantly disagree about the same thing, switch roles for a few minutes. Chris can pretend to be you and you pretend to be Chris. Now talk about the problem as the other person. Hearing Chris tell you how you sound might point out problems with communication. Can you now understand the other person's viewpoint better?

## #11 Set an Example; Be a Role Model

Disappointments happen. That's natural. Show Chris how to easily change plans. When it rains on picnic day, dine on the living room floor, play games and still have fun. The weather is not an excuse to cancel the good time.

> You can't be one kind of person and another kind of parent.
>
> Dr. Phil McGraw
> "Family First"

"Children need parents who model self-discipline rather than preach it," assesses John Bradshaw, *Homecoming*. "They learn from what their parents actually do; not from what they say they do."

Are you self-destructive? Do you smoke, drink in excess, use drugs, date scary people, have scary friends, get arrested or carry weapons? Is that the future you want for Chris? Clean up your act.

➤ Demonstrate self control including controlling when you're happy and when you're sad.

➤ Show Chris how you expect and demand to be treated correctly. Don't let anyone mistreat you.

## #12 Apologize; Be Forgiving

> Any fool can criticize, condemn and complain — and most fools do. But it takes character and self-control to be understanding and forgiving.
>
> Dale Carnegie
> *How to Win Friends & Influence People*

> When you overreact, apologize.
>
> Ross Campbell
> "How to Really Love Your Teenager"

Avoid using guilt as a tool to control Chris. Accept "I'm sorry" from Chris. Talk with her about her plan to change her behavior so it won't happen again. Give her the responsibility to find a solution. Let her lead the discussion about different choices she could make.

**Does Chris think it's easier to ask forgiveness than to get permission?**

Forgive the action but still apply consequences for misbehavior, directs Dr. Phil. Review the rules to see if you are too strict by not allowing her to have any fun from her viewpoint.

## #13 Warn; Give Second Chances

Let Chris know ahead of time that her behavior will result in a consequence:

*My father has the largest hands I have ever seen. When I was a child, my family took many car trips during summer vacations. We three kids sat in the backseat on those hot summer days before air conditioning. As we tried to amuse ourselves, it wasn't an uncommon experience to suddenly have Dad's hand reach from the front seat as he drove and slap one of us. Sometimes, we didn't even know why. Little was learned from such punishment, except I hate long car trips, and my father has the largest hands of any man I know.*

Ginny, mother of 3

A slap with no explanation is just a slap for no reason. It's important that Chris learns from your choice of discipline.

### Are you in a bad mood? Warn your child

An aunt has a special doll in her kitchen. The doll has 3 sides: a happy face, sad face and a frown. To warn her children, she turned the face out that matched her mood for the day. Her children learned how to approach her and when to leave her alone. It also helped them understand that they have bad moods, too.

If every day is a bad day, seek help by talking to your doctor or a professional counselor to uncover more good days.

Julie A. Ross, *Practical Parenting for the 21st Century*, addresses:

Warnings help a child to make sense out of what seems, much of the time, to be a very chaotic and arbitrary [random] existence. They give the child

a sense of order, avoid unpleasant surprises, and
give him a feeling of control — things are not
being done to him, but with him.

## Hand signs warn of inappropriate behavior

Let Chris know that you want to help him behave
appropriately. Say, "I understand that sometimes
it's difficult to keep under control when playing at
Grandma's." When you say his name he is to look at you so
he can see your signal.

☞ Place your index finger on your lips to tell him he is
too loud.

☞ Pat your upper chest a couple of times to tell him he is
acting too wild.

What other signs can Chris and you think of to help?
There will be times when you might suggest that Chris play
outside for awhile so you can visit with the adults. Most
children love to be outside.

The signals show Chris that you respect him and help
him to keep his dignity intact.

## Set a timer and tell Chris how many minutes you set it

✓ Tell Chris supper will be ready in 10 minutes.

✓ We will be leaving the house in 15 minutes.

✓ Bedtime in 30 minutes.

✓ Toys need to be off the floor and put away before the
buzzer rings in 10 minutes (or longer if needed).

## Grant second chances

When you make a mistake, don't you deserve a second
chance? So does Chris. He needs to realize the trust lost
today can be regained. It isn't hopeless. Chris isn't an angel,
but he's also not the devil. Give him another try.

➤ For children under age 5, a few minutes to an hour
later is enough lapse of time for a second chance.

➤ For children age 5 and up, tomorrow or later in the
week is time to try again.

I kept grounding teen Austin from his favorite hangouts — *for life*! That left him with no hope to enjoy his life as he knew it. He also feared I would never trust him again. Big mistake on my part. We all need to know we can correct our mistakes of the past — that there is hope for a bright future.

## #14  Offer Choices

Give choices — if they refuse to choose, that is their choice. There may be consequences for that.

You are preparing Chris for the adult world. Little choices, little steps turn into big choices and risky steps as an adult.

*Choice*: For 30 minutes, you can read a book or write in your journal, before we turn on the TV.

*Choice*: Pick up the toys on your bedroom floor now or after lunch, before you play outside.

*Choice*: Do you want to wear the striped shirt or the button-down today?

☞ Compliment children on their good choices. It's not necessary to bring attention to their bad choices.

### Don't provide excuses for poor behavior choices

*Excuse*: "Poor child. I understand what you're going through."

➤ But she still needs to behave.

*Excuse*: "I don't spend enough quality time with her."

➤ All the more reason she needs to control her emotions and actions so she has lots of good friends.

*Excuse*: "There isn't enough money to provide for all of her needs."

➤ An excuse for irresponsibility? No way!

*Your child's excuse*: "I can't help myself."

➤ Your response might be: "Then let's sit down and discuss ways for you to get better control." This puts Chris in charge of her choices.

### Don't ask, "Why?"

School psychologist Sal Severe says to ask What? — What did she do? Not why did she do it. Have her explain in her terms. Then you can ask, "What could you have done so you would not be in trouble now?" Discuss with your child the correct positive behavior that would have been a better choice.

### Negotiate

Bill O'Reilly offers guidance to children in his book, *The O'Reilly Factor for Kids*, that is also good advise to adults: Recognize "that other people in your life have just as much right to their ways of doing things as you do." Learn "to choose which disagreements are important and which can be settled by compromise," he advises.

Dr. Phil comments, "You teach people how to treat you, and this includes the way you relate to your children. If you don't like your relationship with a child, you need to renegotiate it."

Children want and need some control and some power in matters that affect them directly. He adds, "That is the natural order of things...the rhythm of life."

### Six steps to negotiate successfully

1. First identify what it is that each side seeks out of the negotiation. *For example*: Teen Chris wants a later curfew. You want to know he is safe and behaving responsibly.
2. Avoid the use of manipulation from either side.
3. Wait to negotiate when emotions are calm and all parties are thinking clearly, rationally.
4. Seek a solution that both sides can agree upon.
5. Be specific in the agreement reached and what you expect to happen.
6. Write the negotiated agreement, such as a new curfew for 2 weeks. Once that plan is successful, try a longer time period. If the agreement is not kept, then renegotiate — start over with Step #1.

## #15 Be Fair; Be Respectful

*Fairness. Match punishment with seriousness of problem.*
*Usually grounding was most effective. Respect each other and*
*adults. Apologize when you make a mistake. Discuss problems*
*in privacy of our home. No question is stupid.*

Susan, mother of 3

As Susan states the punishment must equal the crime. If
you go berserk every time Chris doesn't act perfectly, then
he won't know what is important and what is not.

Refuse to put Chris in situations he isn't ready to
handle, such as sitting in church for an hour. When you
know the child's nap time is soon, don't take him
shopping. If you keep him up too late at night, accept
his irritable behavior in the morning. Don't punish him
— that was your mistake.

Children try to make sense of their world and want
everything to be fair. The discipline you choose must be
fair and seem sensible to your child, states Dr. Severe.
If you choose to humiliate, embarrass, intimidate, or
criticize your child, you will damage your relationship
and your child's sense of self worth. Children get revenge
or argue if they feel you've been unjust with punishment.
"Punishment should be mild," Severe reminds us, "to teach
your child to make better decisions."

- Don't pamper or treat Chris like a two-year-old when
  she is ten.
- Speak to Chris in a respectful tone. Avoid using foul
  language. Biting remarks or sarcasm don't remind
  Chris how much you love her.
- Remember, Chris has dignity. Private matters that
  might embarrass her are not to be shared with others.
- Get in her face, eye to eye, and tell her when she is
  misbehaving. Educate Chris so she knows what's
  expected.
- Leave her dignity intact.

When Chris speaks to you rudely, tell him, "I'll listen to you when you can be respectful to me." Then walk away. If you reward this behavior with a burst of angry response, he will feel power over you. Also make sure you don't hear yourself when he talks that way. Are you rude and flippant to Chris? To others?

Teach Chris to respect himself. A child who has self-respect won't get into trouble. If he truly respects himself, why would he be involved in self-destructive behaviors such as the use of illegal drugs, tobacco, risky sexual behavior, or criminal acts?

## #16 Use Humor Appropriately, not Harshly

Humor can sometimes defuse a situation. Laugh at yourself when you make mistakes. Comment on the silly thing you did. Your children will see that they don't have to be perfect, either.

Don't get into the habit of using humor all the time. An inappropriate laugh, or even smile, can make Chris angrier than she was before. Chris wants and needs to be taken seriously.

## #17 Encourage Responsibility

*I instructed them to take responsibility for their mistakes.*
Linda, mother of 3 boys

☞ Children need to be accountable for their actions even if they see others get away with incorrect behavior.
☞ Don't take over your child's responsibilities because you can do it better, or because she forgets.
☞ Tell Chris, that sometimes you say no because of the situation, not because you think she is irresponsible.

### "It's not my fault!"

If Chris always blames misbehavior on someone else, is she learning the pattern from you? Next time you have

> **Do nothing regularly for people that they can do for themselves.**
>
> Rudolf Dreikurs and Vicki Soltz "Children: The Challenge"

a bad day, listen to yourself when you complain about it to anyone within earshot. Do you blame someone else when something doesn't go your way?

## Don't come to the rescue every time

Parents need to squelch the urge "to intervene with a quick fix for every tough assignment or disappointment," lectures Sarah Baldauf, "It's Tough, but You Can Do It" (*U.S. News & World Report*):

A student who misses the year-end spelling prize because he chose not to study has an opportunity to develop thicker skin and learn an important lesson in self-discipline, for example — but not if Mom calls up to berate the teacher.

When parents continually rescue Chris, she expects to be rescued and plans for it even as an adult. After all, if she never had to be responsible before, then why now? The excuse, "I can't help myself," is just that, an excuse. Chris needs to experience the consequences of poor choices and incorrect behavior. We become stronger by surviving our mistakes. (If Chris is involved in a high-risk situation, help her find the right help, today.)

## #18 Be Predictable, Be Consistent

Breakfast at 7; lunch at noon; supper at 6. Bedtimes are posted on the kitchen bulletin board. We have House Rules for homework, watching TV and consequences for incorrect behavior.

As the parent, if you don't deliver the predefined consequence, then you show your child that you don't care. Plus it takes away the child's ability to predict your reaction.

Chris will learn by any correction and know what to expect from you if you are consistent. It does help if you and his other parent have similar goals for behavior.

☞ If you give in just once, the child has won. The misbehavior was worth it. He will definitely plan to try it again.

## Choose to not be predictable, sometimes

When attempts to correct behavior and consequences aren't working, make a change.

### Do something different

React in an unexpected manner. Avoid your first impulse that comes to mind. Chris has been watching you since his eyes first focused. He'll know what reaction to expect from you if he misbehaves. If he plans the misbehavior, then he figures he can survive the punishment. React differently. Throw him off guard.

*TOUGHLOVE®* founders Phyllis and David York acknowledge,

If you always respond in the same way your kids will always know which buttons to push to get what they want.

➢ If you usually yell, be quiet.
➢ If you're usually quiet, yell.
➢ If you usually stay involved, withdraw.
➢ If you usually withdraw, get involved.
➢ Be different.
➢ Don't be so predictable.
➢ Someone who is predictable is easily manipulated and managed.
➢ Surprise yourself — you'll see a change immediately.

**Get over it.** Parents feel embarrassed, hurt, and disappointed by their child's misbehavior. Get in control of your own feelings to help Chris learn self-control.

## #19 Don't Bribe; Seldom Use Rewards

Bribes take away any authority you thought you had. "Bribery makes children obnoxious," cautions Dr. Severe.

> The reward for a thing well done, is to have done it.
>
> Ralph Waldo Emerson

Don't bribe a child to behave in the supermarket while you shop. As Chris ages, she will demand more bribes at greater expense for simple correct behavior.

**Don't threaten.** "...idle threats only teach children that mommy and daddy's words can be ignored because they fail to materialize," relates psychologist Kevin Leman.

When my kids did something special, like perform in a play, we often went to the ice cream shop afterwards. It wasn't so much a reward as a celebration of their achievement. Family time.

Clinical psychologist and creator of the SOS education program Lynn Clark has found:

> **Social Rewards** are very effective in strengthening the desirable behavior of both children and adults. Social rewards include smiles, hugs, pats, kisses, words of praise, eye contact, and attention. A hug or a kind word is easy to give. That's good because our children need lots of social rewards to strengthen their appropriate behavior.

## #20 Instill Incentives to Encourage Good Behavior

"Activity incentives are things children want to do," concedes Severe. Does your child like to play video games, chat on the phone or computer, and spend time with friends? Give children a realistic goal to encourage them to accomplish their tasks first. These are not bribes.

What does your child want and what will he work towards? asks Dr. Phil.

☺ Be alone, or for a small child, spend private time with a parent
☺ Go to the mall
☺ Go to the pool or beach
☺ Play with a certain toy
☺ Ride a bike or skateboard
☺ Sleep in late
☺ Host a sleep over with friends
☺ Chat with his friends on the Internet
☺ Watch television

? What others can you think of that would be good incentives?

**Book Resource:**
Dr. Sal Severe lists ideas for incentives for children under 12 and a separate list for children over 12 in his book, *How to Behave So Your Children Will, Too!*

## Establish Consequences for Incorrect Behavior
Members of our SPWISDOM support group share the consequences they used

*Discipline starts when children are small. If they "run" you when they are little, they will when they are older. Children need to know what behavior is inappropriate and that they are not bad, but their behavior is. They also need to know that they are being disciplined because Mom or Dad care and that they are loved.*                    Tracy, mother of 2

Incorrect behavior on a television show may be funny but not appropriate for real life. Explain the difference to Chris.

*Depriving him of a certain toy or privilege, sending him to his room. I once took his bike away for a week when he misbehaved.*

*As he got older disciplining got harder as a single parent.
Sometimes I would get totally frustrated. I talked to my mom
and friends to get me through it.* Stacy, mother of a boy

*Deny them things they care for. It hurt me, but it worked.*
Margaret, mother of 4

*The only thing that worked was isolation (sending them
to their room, away from the rest of the family). If that meant
that I needed to go outside, I did. I also took phone and
television privileges away.* Rhonda, mother of 2 girls

*Extra cleaning chores like yard work, garage cleaning,
washing cars, painting the deck, all these helped mine to be
more careful.* Vicki, mother of 6

*The most effective was taking away privileges like TV
or going to friends. My daughter learned to sneak out of the
house and got around all discipline and punishment no matter
what. My son accepted his and got on with things. Doing extra
chores seemed to be the best. It helped us both.*
Kat, mother of 2

*At night I was always home, no money given, no freedom
to go away. She couldn't escape her punishment.*
Vicky, mother of a girl

*My son was grounded for 2 weeks once and had
to earn the money to pay for damage to someone's
property.* Clyde, father of 2

*Depriving them of something they wanted very
much such as taking away car keys for a month when
picked up for careless driving.* Cathleen, mother of 9

A human being fashions his consequences as surely as he fashions his goods or his dwelling. Nothing that he says, thinks or does is without consequences.

Norman Cousins

Each decision has "a consequence — a result that happens because of that decision," defines Don Dinkmeyer, Sr., co-author, *Parenting Teenagers*:

Consequences aren't punishment.
- They show respect for both you and your teen.
- They fit the misbehavior.
- They are about behavior.
- They are about now and the future — not the past.
- They are firm and friendly.
- They allow choice.

"If a consequence doesn't make sense, what lesson will be learned?" asks Dr. Dinkmeyer.

Teach children consequences so they can handle life. When they know what to expect will happen because of their actions, the world becomes a fair place to live. If you are always surprising them with your reaction and there is no consistency to the rules, then the world is chaotic to them. They become insecure.

Post the list of consequences and the length of time of each consequence in the kitchen next to the family calendar. Or put them in the "Our Family" notebook. When misbehavior happens you can just point at the consequence on the list as a matter-of-fact to show the punishment that will be used. For more information about the "Our Family" notebook, see page 56.

Whenever attempting to change a bad behavior to a better outcome, things will get worse before they get better. Chris will fight with all his might to keep doing it the way he always has. Be persistent about change. Don't weaken. You are right.

## Time-Out works

*Sit in the corner when they were younger (Time-Out).*
Annette, mother of 2 boys

*Time-Out either on a chair or in their room.*
Debra, mother of 3 boys

*I used Time-Outs a lot. Even for me! If I was too upset I would tell them that I was angry and we would discuss a punishment later when I calmed down.*  Carrie, mother of 2

Time-Outs are best used with 2½- to 9-year-olds. Some parents still use them for 12-year-olds.

When you put children in Time-Out for fighting with each other, state: "You may both get up as soon as you give each other permission to get up," suggests Barbara Coloroso, *Kids Are Worth It!*

Older children may be offered "a choice between sitting and walking" as they "calm themselves more easily if they are moving about," teaches Coloroso. "The purpose and the intended result are the same: to calm down and then deal with the original situation."

☞ See Appendix Time-Outs for more information, page 54.

## Use natural and logical consequences

**Natural Consequence** — If you don't wear your raincoat on a rainy day, you get wet.
**Reasonable Consequence** — You show up late for work three times this month, you lose your job.
**Logical Consequence** — The "correction logically fits the nature of the misbehavior," submits Dr. Clark. "When your child sees a clear and reasonable relationship between her bad behavior and the correction, she is more likely to change her behavior."

Young Maria liked to walk in front of me instead of beside me. I had repeatedly told her to stop doing that for fear I would lose her. She finally stopped after she lost me at the county fair for a few minutes. But first, she scolded me for not staying within her eyesight.

**Enforceable Consequence** — What is and isn't enforceable? Telling your child he cannot smoke isn't enforceable unless he spends every minute of every day with you. You can share all the reasons you are against smoking, but it is up to him. Set rules of no smoking in your home and car. No cigarette butts on the sidewalk or lawn. No allowance if the money is spent on cigarettes or other tobacco products.

**Suggestions for consequences for certain acts**
See APPENDIX CONSEQUENCES, page 52 for our ideas.

## Suspend privileges
*Select only one*: Loss of television time, play time, spending time with friends, bike riding, telephone use, video games, computer, toys, or grounded to room or home. Time limit varies with age of child. No longer than two weeks for the oldest child.

Be sure to discuss the misbehavior and consequence afterwards (no lecture). If you just apply the consequence and don't talk about it, then Chris gets off easy. He needs to learn that the behavior choice was wrong and why he received the consequence.

Parents pay therapists to talk to their children about their behavior choices. You can accomplish the same thing for free. Most of the time asking, "Why did you do it?" isn't helpful. Instead ask, "How can you avoid that misbehavior from happening again?" That puts Chris in charge of finding a solution to a problem he created through lack of self-control.

☞ If the misbehavior is related to drug or alcohol use, seek help, now! See page 60 for our book, *Talk to your Teen*.

☞ Do not use going to bed early as a punishment. Bedtime is the relaxing end of the day, pleads Dr. Severe.

### "If you can't do the time, don't do the crime."

A child, well aware of the consequences, may still choose misbehavior. The consequence needs to be increased to fit the Crime of Intent. Explain to that child how his behavior won't work well in society. We all need to learn to follow the rules and laws. When he breaks the law as an adult, he will find a less forgiving judge.

**Be Patient.** Children need more than one correction to change behavior.

A group of young children were discussing birthdays. One boy matter-of-factly said, "I don't want anything for my birthday. My mom will just take it away when I'm bad."

*How sad!* That child has lost hope. Sure, it's easy to punish a child by removing a toy, but it is failing to encourage this child to behave better. He isn't learning anything. Mom should talk to her child. Ask what he is willing to work towards to stop the punishment. Give him control to improve his life.

### What didn't work...

*No grounding, that was punishing me, too!*
Vicki, mother of 6

*Taking keys away only hurt me.*    Karen, mother of 2 boys

*I don't think anything worked: counseling, talking, punishing, nothing! I think he grew out of it.*
Dody, mother of a boy

## #21 Listen To Your Child First, Then Talk

*For discipline I told them I was their parent and to realize what I did was for their own good. I encouraged them to speak up and give me ideas how things could work out better. I still believe if you let a child know you really love them that they will try to please you.*    Tom, father of 3

*With Abby, discussion and logic was most effective. I never grounded her.* Kathy, mother of a girl

*Punishment was to sit and think about what they did. Then they had to tell me why they did it when they knew they weren't supposed to do it.* Clyde, father of 2

*I was not a hitter. I was, and still am, a talker. I can analyze something to death; that is probably what I did.* Patricia, mother of a boy

## Save your breath. Stop lecturing.

Although you have years of experience you want to share, Chris will tune you out after the first line. If you do it often, she will tune you out when you first open your mouth or get your body in "lecture" position. Try other ways to get your point across. Keep it brief. For communication tips, see *Listen More, Talk Less*, page 60.

*Use Your Words* — a common phrase heard at the play park by parents of young children. When Chris is upset, teach her to use words to explain what is wrong. Then praise her for finding the right words. (Just slowing her thoughts down to find the right words can calm her. Don't rush her.) Teach Chris the appropriate words to express her thoughts and feelings.

☞ Don't ask what happened or why. The story doesn't matter. What does matter is that Chris learns self control and makes wise choices in the future.

"An angry child never hears what anyone has to say until he is allowed to say what he thinks," reveals Marguerite Kelly, "Family Almanac" (*Des Moines Register*).

### Put the "I" in your message, explains Dr. Gordon.

1. Describe "the unacceptable behavior"
2. Say how it makes you feel, and
3. Say exactly what effect it has on you:
   "behavior + feeling + effect"

*Sample I-message*: (1) By missing your curfew, (2) I worry that you are not safe. (3) I can't go to sleep until I know you are safely home.

    "When parents and children learn to be open and honest with each other, they no longer are 'strangers in the same house,'" shares Dr. Gordon.

**Don't assume** you know why Chris is behaving badly or is fearful. Children are exposed to a variety of influences you may not even know about. Talk calmly to her without judgment and without the *I-know-it-all* attitude. Find out if her interpretation of something she overheard or what a friend said is accurate or exaggerated.

### Pay attention to your body language, tone of voice, and expressions

    Use a polite voice when talking to Chris and teach Chris to do the same with you. I have heard the harshest words spoken between parent and child. Teach Chris to talk politely when asking for something or even to tell you she is angry. Say, "I'll wait until you calm down and then we can talk about it." Show respect.

> If problems are all you ever talk about in a relationship, you'll likely have a problem relationship.
>
> Dr. Phil McGraw
> "Family First"

### Listen

    "Being a good listener means hearing beyond the words," instructs Dr. Severe.

    "Do not respond with criticism, judgment, or advice. Keep your opinion to yourself until your child wants to listen. Then use guiding questions to teach your child to think for himself."

## Journal

When Chris is calm, suggest she keep a notebook to write her thoughts when she's out of control. This should be handwritten, not typed on the computer. By actually writing her thoughts on paper her brain will slow down her emotion and focus on the act of writing. She will naturally calm herself. Don't read her journal unless she gives you permission. Even with permission, you may choose to not read it and let her keep the thoughts to herself. Of course, if her room starts filling up with guns and ammunition, or she becomes sexually active, then read everything you can find in her room.

## Write messages

*I found if there were chores that needed to be done, I left a note while I was at work. There seemed to be fewer complaints and usually the chores were done.*        Dorothy, mother of 4

*Delegate, delegate, delegate! Listing jobs on frig worked for awhile. Always write things down you want done by your children. They cannot "forget" that way.*  Meredith, mother of 2

*I always made a list of what chores each child was to do after school and they were very good at finishing the job. They got an allowance and I gave them extra for jobs they did that they did on their own.*        Tom, father of 3

When you are upset at your teen's behavior or actions, write a note to her. Either discuss it with her, or tear it up. I suggest tearing it up. I wrote several letters to my teens and handed them to the child or slipped them under the bedroom door. Reflecting back, that was a bad idea. I could have written the letter to relieve my personal frustration and then torn it up. I should not have given it to my teen. Especially since I didn't encourage discussing the matter later. All my anger and frustration was poured into the words, and then I left my child to handle it, alone. One-sided communication seldom helps any situation.

**IF** only I knew then...

# #22 Don't Punish, Slap, Spank, or Hit

*I only spanked my boys once.*     Annette, mother of 2 boys

*When my children were small I occasionally swatted them on their bottom if they were doing something wrong. This got their attention. Sometimes even small children can have such concentration on a target (like following a ball into the street or grabbing something hot) that a little swat brings them back to reality. Then I explained to them what they were doing wrong and what I wanted them to do right.*

Ginny, mother of 3

Psychologist Kevin Leman shares his concerns about punishment:

> Spanking should be avoided at any cost....the only good that a spanking does is to relieve the parent of the tensions that have built up in him....An occasional swat on a child's 'bummy' is a very good disciplinary measure. In situations where a child's safety is in question, a swat is most appropriate.... Swats always need to be followed up with honest communication expressing our concern and love for the child.

 Thank goodness for enlightenment. I remember as a child waiting for Dad to come home. Then my sister and I would line up for him to spank us on our bottoms. What a horrible task for a parent to face after a day at work. How do you build a loving relationship with that greeting? It didn't deter us from being bad. Mom could have put us in Time-Out for better, immediate discipline.

## Stop child abuse

**I will not treat a child in a way I myself**
**would not want to be treated.**

Barbara Coloroso

Coloroso continues,

> Physical punishment is an obvious form of
> abuse. Not-so-obvious and often-overlooked
> forms of abuse are emotional battering
> and neglect. When children hear constant
> criticism and put downs, they begin to see
> themselves as not good enough or just plain bad.

If you ever think you might hurt your child, call for help. If you see or suspect a child is being abused, call the local police or Child Protective Services. That child needs your help.

CHILDHELP USA National Child Abuse Hotline 1-800-4-A-CHILD (1-800-422-4453), website www.childhelp.org for local contacts. Also check the SINGLE PARENT WISDOM website at www.singleparentwisdom.com, Resources.

## Don't accept parent abuse

When two or more people live together, disagreements happen. That's normal. "Conflict becomes abusive when one person uses threats, force or manipulation to gain power over the other," discloses Barbara Cottrell, Family Violence Prevention Unit, Health Canada, "Parent Abuse: The Abuse of Parents by Their Teenage Children":

> **Parent abuse** is any act of a child that is
> intended to cause physical, psychological or
> financial damage to gain power and control
> over a parent....Abusive behavior should not be
> tolerated.
>
> Some adolescent behavior is more
> irresponsible and thoughtless than abusive....
> While most teens try to persuade their parents
> to provide them with the latest in brand-name
> goods, some abusive teens capitalize on their
> parents' feelings of obligation and inadequacy by
> attempting to force them to spend far more than
> they can afford.

To stop it, you need to realize you are not alone. Seek counseling for you and your child; call the police; talk to someone. Boys Town offers a Hotline 1-800-448-3000.
*Do something!*

## #23 Love Your Child Unconditionally

"Little kindnesses go a long way toward building relationships of trust and unconditional love," finds Stephen R. Covey, an authority on families.

**Unconditionally**, you love your child no matter his good parts, his bad parts, and the wish-he-were-different parts.
"This does not mean that you always like his behavior," offers Dr. Campbell.
**Conditional Love**: I love them only when they please me, and that's the only time I tell them or show my love. When love is based on meeting certain conditions, children will "feel insecure, damage their self-image, and actually prevents them from developing more mature behavior," reports Campbell.

With **Unconditional Love**, children "feel good about themselves and are comfortable with themselves," Campbell concludes. "They will be able to control their anxiety and, in turn, their behavior, as they grow into adulthood."

### Every day, show and tell your child you love her...

A few of the "31 Ways to Tell Your Child I Love You," from Terri Mauro, About.Com: Parenting Special Needs:

☺ Spend a little time each day playing entirely at your child's direction.
☺ Cuddle up under a blanket and watch what he or she wants to watch on TV.
☺ Give a chocolate kiss along with a real one.
☺ Exchange butterfly kisses or nose-to-nose Eskimo kisses.

## #24  Involve the Other Parent, When Possible

Discuss with your child's other parent the expectations you have for how your child should behave. Without your child present, agree on discipline for a few of the basic problems. This is especially important if you live in different homes. You don't want your child taking advantage of the separation. Learning to manipulate adults should seldom be rewarded.

*We had joint custody and every other week switched. If they said, "Mom would let me," or vice versa, sometimes we would call the other parent for support.*     Diane, mother of 2

## #25  Ask For Help Until You Get It

*As a small child, he was very loving, thoughtful and well behaved. As a teen he was a complete turnaround (i.e., drugs, alcohol, smart mouth, etc.). Everything I was not! We went to some counseling.*     Dody, mother of a boy

*We went to family counseling, the boys went to counseling. I did everything I could.*     Debra, mother of 3 boys

Debra had difficulty with her ex and the negative things he continually told their boys about their mother to damage their relationship. With hard work and self reflection, you can change your behavior. You can guide your child towards the correct choices to change his behavior. You cannot change another adult's behavior — they need to change for themselves. When the other parent, relatives, or friends misbehave, protect your child by reducing the amount of contact with that person when possible. You may have to involve the court system.

### Would you or your child benefit from an Anger Management workshop?

Call the local hospital or social service agency to find a class in your area.

## Be a support system for your child

Chris needs to feel comfortable coming to you with a problem. The goal of bad behavior may be an attempt to get your attention so the two of you can discuss the real problem.

Chris needs to have friends her own age. It's also helpful for her to get to know her other relatives. If Chris has other adults that she can confide in, it will relieve her of the burden of protecting you from disappointment with her.

## Find a support system for yourself

You need someone you can call when you cannot figure out what to do about Chris. Or just find someone to agree with you that raising children is a tough job. Is there a relative or a close friend you can call? Are there recreational clubs in your area where you can be you and not a parent for a few hours?

Talk to the reference librarian at your town library to see if there are such clubs. What support groups already exist in your area for specific problems?

*When I look back and reflect on the challenge I faced, it was overwhelming. Regrets, of course, for my impatience and yelling at times instead of creating special moments to sit*  *down and talk over the problem, to find solutions and discuss our emotions, etc. I wish I had tried to create more story times or occasions to air our frustrations. I guess I thought I had to fix everything. I thought I had to keep wading through it all. When I reflect on all the tears and regrets, I realize I've been blessed beyond belief with so many gifts, my children, my friends, financial security, etc. The everyday miracles and rainbows get overlooked sometimes if I don't take the time to pray and reflect. I believe I've grown stronger as a person because of all the trials.*

Marge, mother of 9

# 25 Ways to
# Encourage Good Behavior

1. Take Care of Problems Now, Not Later
2. Provide Structure and Boundaries
3. Set Positive, Reachable Goals
4. Find Your Strength
5. Be More Positive, and Less Negative
6. Praise, Encourage, Appreciate
7. Be Patient, Be Affectionate
8. Distract or Redirect
9. Remove Yourself from the Situation
10. Role-play
11. Set an Example, Be a Role Model
12. Apologize, Be Forgiving
13. Warn, Give Second Chances
14. Offer Choices
15. Be Fair, Be Respectful
16. Use Humor Appropriately, Not Harshly
17. Encourage Responsibility
18. Be Predictable, Be Consistent
19. Don't Bribe, Seldom Use Rewards
20. Instill Incentives to Encourage Good Behavior, & Consequences for Incorrect Behavior
21. Listen to Your Child First, Then Talk
22. Don't Punish, Slap, Spank, or Hit
23. Love Your Child Unconditionally
24. Involve The Other Parent, When Possible
25. Ask for Help

## Appendix: Consequences

Suggested consequences for certain acts
    Adapt these to fit Chris to his current age, ability, and the situation. Children learn from properly applied consequences. You judge the situation and decide if the consequence is fair. For first time offenses, like oversleeping and missing the school bus, please be more easy-going. Your goal is to teach Chris to be responsible (within his ability at his age). After applying an action, always discuss the misbehavior and consequence with Chris after everyone cools down. Don't lecture.

☞ *Draws on wall* — Natural consequence is for the child to clean up the mess. Child washes the wall that was drawn on. Instruct on the proper way to do it, or help. Caution: If the cleanup is fun, he'll do it again. Repaint if needed.

☞ *Mess up a room or area* — Clean it up before child can leave house, watch television, or go to bed.

☞ Backtalk/Disrespect — Child needs to show respect to you. Child is removed from society (sent to bedroom) or Time-Out. He loses your friendship and cooperation for a half hour (really small child); a few hours (small child); a day (older child). Chris will learn he needs your friendship and cooperation to go through the day.

☞ Uses foul language — Put 25 cents in the Penalty Jar or Time-Out. If it doesn't stop — No TV for the day.

☞ Hits a friend, sibling or you — Time-Out

☞ Lies to you — Needs to show you respect and to trust you with the truth. Talk about his choice to lie. Although it can be difficult to know for sure if it is a lie, since Chris will most likely not confess. You can discuss with him the fear you have that he isn't telling you the truth to you. Suggest he convince you he is.

☞ Fights over the television — Loss of privileges, such as no TV for a few hours, or day. Redirect to something else.

☞ When siblings fight — Time-Out for both, then not allowed to play together for #___hours.

☞ Misses supper by coming home too late — Eats leftovers or has to fix own meal. Cleans up his supper dishes.

☞ Forgets school lunch or lunch money (not first time) — Goes hungry (or talks a friend into sharing).

☞ Forgets gym clothes or school books (not first time) — Suffers the consequences from the teacher.

☞ Oversleeps and misses the school bus (not first time) — If it's a safe neighborhood and the school is within a mile, he walks to school.

☞ Fails to show up for an appointment (like the orthodontist) — He reschedules the appointment making own arrangements to get there.

☞ Fails to complete assigned household chores — Must complete chore before leaving home. Loss of privileges: such as a ride to the mall or friend's house, or movies with friends this weekend.

☞ Dishes not cleaned from previous meal by person assigned to do the task — No meal preparation until the dishes are clean and put away. Discuss the problem while doing the dishes with your children, or after the children have done them.

☞ Spends all his money — natural consequence of no more money to spend.

☞ Leaves the house instead of following the consequence — Has to do whatever she was supposed to do before she can join the family again. No TV. No cooperation from others until followed.

☞ Returns home after curfew — Curfew moved up that amount of time — late by 30 minutes, curfew 30 minutes earlier; late by an hour, curfew moved up an hour, etc. Discuss with her why she has a curfew: safety, sleep is important, town curfew.

☞ Sneaks out after bedtime — Loss of privileges: Can't go out with friends or family the next day, or next weekend.

☞ Fails to show up for work on time — Loses the job. Don't provide excuses or lie for him. I know a parent's natural instinct is to protect our young (even if he is taller than us). If you child has a job, he needs to accept the responsibility of keeping it.

☞ Damages someone's property — Pays for the damage (needs to find a job or way to earn the money to pay the damages). Physically repairs the damage, if possible, such as remove graffiti and paint again. Discuss the rights of the person whose property was damaged and the rights Chris is losing because of his behavior choice.

☞ Gets a ticket for speeding or other poor driving — Pays the fine and increase in insurance premiums. Loses driving privileges for a set amount of time.

☞ Damages the car — Pays for the repairs and loses driving privileges for a set amount of time.

☞ Gets arrested — Pays the bail and fines. Finds own attorney, who he also pays. Discuss your child's choices that ended up in the arrest and how he can change his behavior.

# APPENDIX: TIME-OUTS

## Time-Out works

Time-Outs are best used with 2 ½- to 9-year-olds. Some parents still use them with 12-year-olds.

**Guidelines to find a good location for Time-Out:**
- ✓ Small child — must be within your eyesight
- ✓ NO closets or dark rooms!
- ✓ No possibility of playing while in Time-Out. Boring, but safe.
- ✓ No siblings or friends nearby to make faces at.
- ✓ No television to watch.
- ✓ No window to look out. (Although some people think this is too harsh.)
- ✓ Nothing dangerous or breakable within reach of child. (That's why I disagree with using a bathroom for Time-Out — automatic flood zone!)

## How much time for a Time-Out?

No more than one minute for every year of the child's life. Any more than that is cruel punishment.

Ages 2 and 3: 1 or 2 minutes
Ages 3 to 5: 2 or 3 minutes
Age 5: 5 minutes
Age 6: 6 minutes, and so on

## Use a timer

A portable timer removes the blame from you for setting the time limit in the first place. The timer starts when the child is calm, and remains calm. Ignore her during this time.

**Important:** After the Time-Out is served, discuss the reason for it. Explain what behavior is expected. Be brief.

☞ If Chris doesn't accept Time-Out, then you need another plan. Don't leave her there for more than 3 times the original amount of time.

## Use Time-Out to reduce these types of misbehaviors:

- arguing
- swearing
- fighting
- hitting
- talking back
- disobedience (not doing what she is told)

Don't use Time-Out for every misbehavior. Be creative. Use Time-Out for behaviors you are trying to change. Explain to Chris why he was disciplined.

**Time-Out is not effective for the following behaviors**
Lynn Clark, *SOS Help for Parents*, spells them out for us:
- ☹ Pouting, sulking
- ☹ Irritableness, bad moods, grumpiness
- ☹ Failing or forgetting to do chores
- ☹ Failing to pick up clothes and toys
- ☹ Not doing homework or piano practice
- ☹ Fearfulness
- ☹ Being dependent, timid or passive
- ☹ Seclusiveness, wanting to be alone
- ☹ Overactive behavior (but *do* Time-Out aggressive or destructive acts)
- ☹ Behaviors not observed by the parents [heresay]

**Time-Outs can work when you are away from home**
- When you're in the car: Car seat
- When you're waiting at the doctor's: Chair in doctor's waiting room
- When you're at the grocery store: Café chair at grocery store or clean corner
- When you're at someone's home visiting: Safe, boring location

**The need for Time-Outs should become less**
If there is no improvement, then the correction isn't working. Tell Chris that you are concerned that he isn't learning to control himself. He has too many Time-Outs. Assure him you know he can do this and ask for his cooperation to learn self-control. This will allow him more independence. Choose a different consequence.

When you put children in Time-Out for fighting with each other, state: "You may both get up as soon as you give each other permission to get up," suggests Barbara Coloroso, *Kids Are Worth It!*
Older children may be offered "a choice between sitting and walking" as they "calm themselves more easily if they are moving about," teaches Coloroso. "The purpose and the intended result are the same: to calm down and then deal with the original situation."

# Appendix: "Our Family" Notebook

## Organize with information in one place

First, get a 3-ring binder. Find a place to keep it in your kitchen. Store family information:

> *Contact Information*: Phone numbers of your work, relatives, friends, neighbors, emergency contacts
> Your child's school calendar
> Schedules of any other activities for your child or you, such as music or art classes
> Your child's sports team calendar and phone numbers of teammates
> *Food*: Menus for dinner, Freezer contents, Grocery Shopping List*
> *Household Chores Task List**
> *Financial Management*: Budget Tables*, Bills due list [You may want to keep this information in a place where others do not see it.]
> *Health Information:* Allergies, medicines, prescription information
> *Medical Authorization Form** one completed for each child
> *Discipline Guidelines*, House Rules, consequences,
> *Babysiter Notes*: Your home address, phone numbers of fire and police, child's fears, and what you want the babysitter to do in your absence, such as wash dishes used, bedtime routine (bedtimes and how many stories to read, snacks, bath tonight?)
> *Auto Care Records*: Last oil change, repairs made
> *Safety*: Fire evacuation plan for each room of the house
> Plus whatever else you want to have in one easy access location.

## *Make It Easy on Yourself*

Order a start-up "Our Family" notebook:

> Receive a 1" 3-ring binder with insertable front cover & 2 pockets
> Index separators with tabs
> Tabs: Auto, meals, household chores, sports, babysitter form, consequences, grocery shopping list, budget
> Pocket separators

Send $22.95 (includes shipping to U.S. addresses) to "Our Family" Notebook, Wynot Publications, PO Box 477, Corning, IA 50841 or order using the last page of this book.

*Forms available for download at the singleparentwisdom.com website, Forms

Copyright 2009 Wynot Publications

# Index

**A-B**
abuse 46, 47
adolescence; See teens
age-appropriate 2, 11-12, 16, 30, 53
alcohol 41, 49
allowance 41, 45
anger 7, 18, 20, 24, 26, 33, 40, 43-45, 49
anxiety 48
apologize 32
appreciation 21, 23, 51
argues 32, 51
attention 18, 22, 24, 36, 44, 46, 50
attitude 20, 44
authority 36, 48
babies 4, 22
backtalk 52
bedroom 11, 15-17, 41, 45, 52-53
boundaries 8, 13-14, 51

**C**
calendar 11, 39, 56
car 22, 26, 38, 41, 53
celebrate 22
chaos 2, 8-9, 19, 29, 47
child abuse 46
choices 2, 7, 13, 18, 27-8, 30-1, 34, 39-41, 43, 49, 51-3
chores 10-11, 16, 38, 45, 53
communication, see listening, talking
computers 36-7, 41, 45
confidence 20
conflict 47
consequences 7, 10-11, 14, 16, 18, 25, 28, 30, 34-5, 37-42, 51-3
consideration 10, 23
consistency 1, 13-14, 19, 34, 39, 51
control 17-18, 21, 27, 29-31, 35, 41-3, 45, 48
cooperation 21, 23, 52-3
counseling 28, 41-2, 48-9
crisis/tragedy 2, 8-9, 19, 47
curfew 9-10, 31, 44, 53

**D-E-F**
dating 9, 27
decision making 1, 11-12, 32, 38
depression 18
drugs 27, 33, 41, 49
encouragement 13, 16, 19, 21, 23, 33, 36, 42-3, 45, 51
expectations 11, 49
fairness 7, 10, 32, 39, 40, 51-2
family fun 13, 15, 27
family meetings 13, 16
fear 14, 32, 40, 44, 52
fighting 8, 10-11, 40
forgetting 18, 45
forgive 27-8, 42, 51
foul language 32, 52
friendship 10, 12, 16-17, 26-7, 30, 37-8, 41, 44, 49-50, 52-3, 56
frustration 18, 25, 38, 45
future 3, 5, 8, 27, 30, 39, 42-3

**G-H**
games 12, 27, 36, 41
goals 15, 18, 23, 34, 36, 50-2
guidelines 13, 24
guilt 27
happiness 21, 27, 33
homework 15, 21, 34
honesty 9, 44, 46
household chores 11, 16, 53
house rules 7, 9-10, 14, 16, 34, 38, 44-5, 53

**I-J-K-L**
incentives 15
kitchen 10, 39
laughter 33, 52
laws 9-10, 31, 44, 53
listening 1, 12, 14, 17, 19-20, 33-4, 42-4, 52

**M-N**
manipulation 9, 31, 35, 47, 49
mental health 18, 48-9
money 38, 41, 52-3

mornings 3, 11, 16
music 25
nature 40
negative 15, 19-21, 49, 51
negotiate 31

**O-P**
"Our Family" notebook 39, 56
overwhelmed 25, 50
parent, other 34, 49, 51
parent abuse 47
patience 4, 18, 24, 42, 51
perfectionism 22, 33
phone 17, 36, 38, 41, 56
positive 15, 19-20, 31, 51
praise 16, 19, 21, 36, 43
privacy 32, 37
privileges 15, 38, 41-2, 52-3
punishment 18, 28, 32, 35, 38, 40-3,
    46-7, 52

**Q-R**
reading 19, 30, 45
relatives 49-50, 56
resentment 7
resources 5, 37, 47
respect 9, 12, 17, 29, 32-3, 39, 44, 51-2
responsibility 1, 3, 25, 27, 33-4, 51-3
revenge 18, 32
rewards 15-16, 33, 36, 51
risks 30, 33-4
role models 3, 27, 51
role play 26, 51
routine 8, 16
rules 7-14, 16, 18, 24-5, 28, 34, 39, 41-2

**S**
safety 10, 14, 33-4, 46, 53
school 8-11, 18, 22, 26, 52-3, 56
second chances 29, 51
security 14, 50
self control 17-18, 24, 27, 29-31, 35,
    41-3, 45, 48
self talk 19
sharing 23, 37, 41, 43
shopping 22, 32, 36
sleep 17, 18, 37, 44, 53
smoking 33, 41
stress 18-19
structure 1-2, 8, 51
support 5, 49-50

**T**
talking 8, 11-14, 16-29, 32-3, 40-4, 48,
    50, 52
teamwork 21, 23, 52-3
teens 2, 9, 13, 16, 23, 31, 39, 45, 49
telephone 17, 36, 38, 41, 56
television 10-11, 37-8, 41, 48, 52-3
therapy 42, 48-9
threats 36, 47
Time-Out 10, 40, 46, 52, 54
TOUGHLOVE® 35
trust 29-30, 48, 52

**U-V-W**
unconditional love 48, 51
understanding 20, 27
violence 47
warnings 8, 12, 20, 28-9, 51
websites 23, 47, 59
wisdom 5, 23, 30, 37, 47, 59
work 4, 19, 22, 38, 40, 42, 45-6, 50, 53

# BIBLIOGRAPHY

➤ **Boys Town** hotline 1-800-448-3000; website www.boystown.org; parenting tips website parenting.org

➤ *Family First: Your Step-By-Step Plan for Creating a Phenomenal Family* by Phil McGraw (NY: Free Press)

➤ *How to Behave So Your Children Will, Too!* by Sal Severe (NY: Viking Penguin)

➤ *How to Really Love Your Teenager* by Ross Campbell (Victor Books)

➤ *Keeping Life Simple: 7 Guiding Principles 500 Tips & Ideas* by Karen Levine (Pownal, VT: Storey Books)

➤ *Kids Are Worth It! Giving Your Child the Gift of Inner Discipline* by Barbara Coloroso (NY: Quill)

➤ *Parent Effectiveness Training, P.E.T.* by Thomas Gordon. (NY: Three Rivers Press)

➤ *Parenthood Without Hassles\* (\*well almost)* by Kevin Leman (Eugene, OR: Harvest House)

➤ *Parenting Teenagers: Systematic Training for Effective Parenting of Teens (S.T.E.P.).* by Don Dinkmeyer, Sr., Gary D. McKay, Joyce L. McKay and Don Dinkmeyer, Jr. (Circle Pines, MN: American Guidance Service)

➤ *Practical Parenting for the 21st Century.* by Julie A. Ross (NY: Excalibur Publishing)

➤ *Simplify Your Life With Kids: 100 Ways to Make Family Life Easier and More Fun* by Elaine St. James and Vera Cole (KC: Andrews McMeel Publishing)

➤ *SOS Help for Parents: A Practical Guide for Handling Common Everyday Behavior Problems* by Lynn Clark Clark, Lynn. (Bowling Green, KY: Parents Press) Several chapters devoted to Time-Out.

➤ *Stress Management for Dummies\** by Allen Elkin (NY: Wiley)

➤ *The O'Reilly Factor for Kids* by Bill O'Reilly and Charles Flowers. (NY: HarperCollins) written for your older child

Find more helpful resources on the **SINGLE PARENT WISDOM** website at singleparentwisdom.com.

# How to Order More
## Other books in the "Single Parent Wisdom" series:
All books are 64 pages and easy to read.

_____ 101. 25 Ways to Encourage Good Behavior
_____ 102. Strong Family, Strong Child
_____ 103. Parents! Take Care of Yourself
_____ 104. How to Make Parental Decisions & Solve Problems
_____ 105. A Day with a Plan is an Easier Day
_____ 106. Get in Control! Feel Emotions, Choose Behavior
_____ 107. Be a Role Model, Share Your Values
_____ 108. Talk to your Teen
_____ 109. Play, Laugh, Share Family Fun
_____ 110. Listen More, Talk Less
_____ 111. Support Learning
_____ 112. Tips to Keep a Tidy Home
_____ 113. Breakfast at 7; Supper at 6
_____ 114. Live Healthy, Stay Well
_____ "Our Family" Notebook Kit $22.95

Only
$9$^{95} each

Order 5 or
more and pay
only $7$^{95} each

__*Quantity Discounts*: Save 20% when you order 5 or more books, any combination (only $7.95 each).

Orders from individuals must be prepaid by check or credit card. Agencies may FAX their purchase orders to 1-816-278-9426. Or order online at www.singleparentwisdom.com. Return Guaranteed if book(s) returned within 30 days of purchase in good condition.

**Order Form:**

Name: _____

Address: _____

City:_____State: _____ Zip: _____

Credit Card (check one):     ___Visa  ___Mastercard  ___Discover

Account #_____Ex. Date_____

_____
Print name as it appears on card.

Daytime Phone (_____)_____
                    (Telephone number needed if credit card used.)
Shipping:  Add $3 for each book ordered, sent First Class (U.S.)
                Add $6 for each book sent Priority Mail (U.S.)
Call for quantity shipping or see Shipping Chart on the website
www.singleparentwisdom.com
Mail this order form to Wynot Publications, P.O. Box 477, Corning, IA 50841